The Nullification Handbook

I0439910

Bert Loftman
Copyright © 2013 Bert Loftman
All rights reserved.

ISBN-13: 978-1484137918

DEDICATION

Bunny Loftman
My patient wife and editor

Thomas Jefferson
Declaration of Independence
The Virginia Resolution

James Madison
U.S. Constitution,
The Kentucky Resolution

TABLE OF CONTENTS

INTRODUCTION

America's future is in doubt. Our economy is faltering, our country is in debt, our money is being inflated, and our Bill of Rights is being corrupted. Most of our federal officials do not serve the public. They often exempt themselves from the laws they make. Most remain in office, lording it over us, until they retire.

It often seems hopeless as we go through the process of electing federal officials who say they believe in a smaller less intrusive government and then vote for bigger government. It is likely hopeless if we continue to follow unconstitutional federal laws. These are often laws that are made by Congress, signed by the President, and ruled constitutional by the Supreme Court. However, as this book will show, these laws are often not constitutional. These three branches of government are not infallible. There is hope, but it does not come from the federal government, it comes from state and local governments.

Ours is a federalist form of government. The Constitution is a contract between the federal government and the states. In this contract, the states surrenders certain powers to the federal government. The states retain all other powers for themselves and for the people. Federalism only works if the states can effectively respond when the federal government makes laws that are not in it its powers to create.

This hand book will guide interested Americans and public servants at the state and local levels on how to create a better future through nullification and interposition. To do this, we must understand the underlying principles of our U.S. Constitution and its built in safeguards to prevent tyranny. Once understood, we can stop blindly following unconstitutional laws.

Chapter 1
NULLIFICATION AND INTERPOSITION
The rightful remedies for
Corruption of The U.S. Constitution

Nullification occurs when a federal law is found not to be pursuant to the Constitution and therefore null and void and not to be followed. This book explains who does the finding and what they can do about it.

Interposition occurs when a state, county, sheriff, or city protects their citizens from the federal government trying to enforce a nullified law.

The U.S. Constitution is the contract between the federal government and the states. The Supremacy Clause says the Constitution is the supreme law of the land when federal laws are pursuant to it, Article VI, Clause 2:

This Constitution, and the Laws of the United States which shall be made in Pursuance thereof ... shall be the supreme Law of the Land;

Often we hear people say, "The laws of the federal government are the supreme law of the land."   They ignore or are ignorant that the Constitution says only laws pursuant to the Constitution are the supreme law of the land.

The Tenth Amendment says:

The powers not delegated to the United States by the Constitution, nor prohibited by it to the States, are reserved to the States respectively, or to the people.

Nowhere in the Constitution does it say that the Supreme Court is the sole judge of whether a federal law is pursuant to the Constitution. The states, counties, sheriffs, and cities also have the power to nullify unconstitutional federal laws.

Thomas Jefferson wrote the Declaration of Independence and said:

He has erected a multitude of New Offices, and sent hither swarms of Officers to harass our people, and eat out their substance.

Today, our country faces many of the same problems. "Eating our their substance" would refer to federal agencies' regulations like:

• The Environmental Protection Agency (EPA) dictating that people could not fill in low areas on their private lands because they are wetlands, even though they are dry most of the time.

- Occupational and Safety and Health Administration (OSHA) dictating expensive regulations, many of which are unnecessary.
- The Food and Drug Administration (FDA) dictating prolonged drug testing that keeps life saving drugs from patients.

Some of the policies of these agencies may necessary, but they are not authorized by the Constitution. Those that are necessary should be implemented at the state level. When special interest groups can lobby our central government for their various causes, they often produce results that are detrimental to society as a whole. This is a dangerous process that leads to violence and tyranny. The original intent of our Constitution was to control the special interest groups or factions by a federation. This book shows how we have abandoned the original intent and the result is central control by the factions.

The Declaration of Independence says:

That whenever any Form of Government becomes destructive of these ends, it is the Right of the People to alter or to abolish it,

This book also explains how our state and local officials can alter our government through the peaceful process of nullification and interposition. Doing this would return us to a federation where the federal government has few powers and the states have many powers.

Chapter 2
THE CONSTITUTION

In 1781, the United States created a Republic. This is a form of government by the people and has no hereditary monarch. The U.S ratified its first constitution, the Articles of Confederation and Perpetual Union. A few years later, George Washington, Alexander Hamilton, and James Madison came to the conclusion that the Articles of Confederation were inadequate. They persuaded the states to hold a Constitutional Convention and this resulted in the writing of the U.S. Constitution. The Convention sent this to the states for ratification.

James Madison, Alexander Hamilton, and John Jay wrote the *Federalist Papers* to explain to the states and the people how this new government would operate.

The Federalist Papers

James Madison is often called the father of our Constitution and wrote the Tenth Federalist Paper, "The Utility of the Union as a Safeguard Against Domestic Faction and Insurrection." This is the most famous of the Federalist Papers where he explained that a major purpose of the U.S. Constitution was to control factions.

Factions are a type of a special interest group who lobby governments to implement their causes. Often these causes are detrimental to society as a whole or to individual liberties. Madison said that factions lobbying a central government, "Have, in truth, been the mortal disease under which popular governments everywhere have perished"

He argued that you could not control the cause of factions because it is "sown in the nature of man." Each of us is endowed with reason, which we use to come to various and often conflicting opinions. People with similar opinions often join forces to become a faction that lobbies government to advance their cause.

Madison therefore concluded that governments cannot control the cause of faction. They can only control its effects. The way to do this is to create a federation of sovereign states forming a federal government with limited and clearly defined powers. He said that with a federation, "The influence of factious leaders may kindle a flame within their particular States, but will be unable to spread a general conflagration through the other States."

He echoed this in the Forty-fifth Federalist Paper:

The powers delegated by the proposed Constitution to the federal government are few and defined. Those which are to remain in the State governments are numerous and indefinite.

In the Thirty-third Federalist Paper, Alexander Hamilton discussed the Supremacy Clause:

But it will not follow from this doctrine that acts of the large society which are NOT PURSUANT to its constitutional powers, but which are invasions of the residuary authorities of the smaller societies, will become the supreme law of the land. These will be merely acts of usurpation, and will deserve to be treated as such.

Hamilton used the term "smaller societies." This implies that states, counties, sheriffs, and cities do not need to follow unconstitutional laws.

The states ratified the Constitution in 1790 and the Bill of Rights came into effect in 1791.

Principles of '98

John Adams was our second President and in 1798, he corrupted the Constitution. He was angered when people called him names such as, "A repulsive pedant, a gross hypocrite and an unprincipled oppressor." Adams had led us into a "Quasi-war" with France and war creates a good excuse to expand government. In 1798, he spearheaded the *Alien and Sedition Acts*. These Acts said it was against the law to criticize the government. This resulted in the arresting of twenty-five and the jailing of ten citizens.

Two of our founding fathers were upset with this and countered with two resolutions known as "The Principles of '98."

Kentucky Resolution

Thomas Jefferson drafted the Kentucky Resolution that he called "The rightful remedy." It called for nullification of unconstitutional federal laws:

That the government formed by the Constitution of the United States was not the exclusive or final judge of the extent of the powers delegated to itself; but that, as in all other cases of compact among parties having no common judge, each party has an equal right to judge for itself, as well of infractions as of the mode and measure of redress."

Virginia Resolution

James Madison wrote The Virginia Resolution on interposition:

The states who are parties thereto, have the right, and are in duty bound, to interpose for arresting the progress of the evil.

The Constitution is a legal contract between the states and the federal government. In a contract with no appointed arbitrator, both members of the contract have an equal right to determine if the contract is broken and make appropriate adjustments. There is nothing in the U.S. Constitution that gives the Supreme Court the exclusive right to nullify unconstitutional laws.

Jefferson and Madison did not go to The Supreme Court lawyers asking them to nullify the Alien and Sedition Acts. They went to the states.

This nullification effort, like most others that followed, ended because the offending federal laws were repealed. Adams was a one term President. When Jefferson took office, he was successful in repealing the Alien and Sedition

Acts. This has been an ongoing pattern where onerous unconstitutional laws are passed and then repealed after a nullification effort.

Constitutional Review by Courts

Marbury v. Madison (1803) is a landmark case where the Supreme Court ruled that the Supreme Court had the power of judicial review over federal laws.

This was a controversial decision because some believed that this might give the Supreme Court too much power. They feared the Supreme Court might strike down constitutional laws and this would defeat the will of the people. This ruling increased the power of the Supreme Court but in an opposite way that they envisioned. The Supreme Court did not rule that constitutional laws were unconstitutional; it began ruling that unconstitutional laws were constitutional.

Marbury v. Madison did not say that the Supreme Court had the sole power to rule a law unconstitutional.

In *United States v. Peters* (1809) the Supreme Court ruled that it did have the sole power to rule a federal law unconstitutional and the states did not have this power to nullify federal laws.

In subsequent cases, the Supreme Court confirmed their belief that they had the sole power of nullification. The Supreme Court consists of nine lawyers who are employed and paid by the Federal Government. When a new justice is needed, they are appointed by whoever happens to be the President at the time. The appointment is then approved or rejected by the Senate. This book later explains how the Supreme Court was corrupted by President Roosevelt with, "A Switch in Time Saves Nine."

The nullification movement understands that the Supreme Court is part of the same federal government that makes and executes its laws. It does not accept that the Supreme Court is the sole judge of federal laws. Nowhere in the Constitution does it say that the Supreme Court has the sole power to rule a federal law unconstitutional.

Current Nullification Efforts

There are many nullification efforts happening throughout the United States. The *TenthAmendmentCenter.com* is an excellent site to learn more about nullification. It has model legislations and describes the status of current and past nullification efforts:

- State Marijuana Laws
- NDAA: Liberty Preservation
- Obamacare
- TSA: Travel Freedom
- 2nd Amendment
- Drones: Privacy Protection
- REAL ID
- Constitutional Tender
- Hemp Freedom Act
- Defend the Guard
- Sheriffs First
- Food Freedom Act
- Intrastate Commerce

CHAPTER 3
CORRUPTION - COMMERCE CLAUSE
Corruption is a deviation from the ideal

Article I, Section 8, Clause 3
To regulate Commerce with foreign Nations, and among the several States;

The financial foundations of central control began in 1913 with the income tax and the Federal Reserve Bank. These financially weaken the American people by discouraging saving making many of them dependent on the federal government. These are the second and fifth planks of <u>The Communist Manifesto</u>:

1. *Abolition of property in land and the application of all rents of land to public purposes*
2. ***A heavy progressive or graduated income tax***
3. *Abolition of all rights of inheritance*
4. *Confiscation of the Property of all Emigrants and Rebels*
5. ***Centralization of credit in the hands of the State***
6. *Centralization of the means of communications and transportation in the hands of the State*
7. *Extension of factories and instruments of production owned by the State*
8. *Equal liability of all to labor. Establishment of industrial armies especially for agriculture*

9. Combination of agriculture with manufacturing industries, gradual abolition of the distinction between town and country, by a more equitable distribution of population over the country

10. Free education for all children in public schools. Abolition of children's factory labor in its present form. Combination of education with industrial production

The income tax discourages savings as shown by the popularity of IRAs and other measures which spare income from taxation. The Federal Reserve Bank fulfills the fifth plank by printing paper money that the federal government spends. This causes inflation to the point that a 1964 dime containing silver was worth $3.50 in 2012. Inflation discourages savings and encourages debt. People in debt are a dependent people.

Keynesian economics theorizes that printing fiat or paper money is good because it dampens the business cycle. If the counterfeiters of The Federal Reserve Bank were angels, this might work but they are not angels. At the very start, they overprinted fiat dollars. This led the United States into the boom known as "The Roaring 20s."

In October of 1929, the boom ended with a stock market crash and this preceded the start of a recession. The government tried to help with the Smoot-Hawley Tariff Act of 1930. This started a global trade war that moved the recession into The Great Depression.

President Franklin D. Roosevelt (FDR) was elected by promising a New Deal that was designed to get us out of the Great Depression. FDR would fix the problems the government caused with a series of legislations, many of which created regulatory programs.

Chapter 4
CORRUPTION - SUPREME COURT
Corruption is a deviation from the ideal

"THE SWITCH IN TIME THAT SAVED NINE"

Initially, the Supreme Court ruled that most of Roosevelt's New Deal programs were unconstitutional. This infuriated FDR and in 1937 he championed The Court Reform Bill. This "reform" would expand the Supreme Court from nine to fifteen members. Of course, Roosevelt would make sure that the six new lawyers would Support his New Deal.

Supreme Court as it would look with 15 members

With this threat, Justice Owen Roberts switched from voting for the Constitution to voting for the New Deal. This corruption of The Supreme Court was known as "The Switch in Time that Saved Nine."

During the Great Depression prices were depressed and farmers were hurting. They formed a faction that lobbied the federal government for relief. In 1938 the government responded with The Agricultural Adjustment Act. This contained wheat quotas which were designed to help farmers by raising the price of wheat.

This raised the price of wheat, but it also evoked The Law of Unintended Consequences. When wheat prices rose, so did the price of bread, which hurt struggling families during The Great Depression. Also, farmers' incomes dropped because the increased price of wheat did not offset their decreased production.

Farmer Roscoe Filburn had a wheat quota of ten acres that he planned to sell on the open market. He also planted more wheat than his quota and planned to use this to feed his chickens.

The U.S. Department of Agriculture fined Farmer Filburn for exceeding his quota. He refused to pay believing that growing wheat to feed his chickens was not "**Commerce with foreign Nations, and among the several States**." After all, the market for wheat crossed national boundaries. The federal government did not dictate to the farmers of foreign nations how much wheat to grow. It seems reasonable that the same rules would apply to Farmer Filburn.

Secretary Wickard, U.S. Department of Agriculture, disagreed and sued Farmer Filburn.

Wickard and Filburn

In 1942, the corrupted Supreme Court ruled against Filburn and the original intent of the Constitution. The Court reasoned that if he had not grown his own wheat, he would have bought it on the open market and this would affect **"Commerce with foreign Nations, and among the several States."**

This ruling legitimized the federal government regulating trade and the production of goods within a state. This ruling set a precedent that has been followed to this day by the Supreme Court and the lower federal courts. The justices of the all the courts take an oath to support the Constitution. They do not take an oath to support the rulings of prior Supreme Courts.

This ruling has created the regulatory state. It gives power to the factions who control the regulatory states, as shown below.

	Factions			
	Legislative	Executive	Judicial	
Federal	Congress	President	Supreme Court	Regulatory Agencies
State	General Assembly	Governor		
Local		Sheriff		

In the Wealth of Nations, Adam Smith said, "It is not from the benevolence of the butcher, the brewer, or the baker, that we expect our dinner, but from their regard to their own interest." This self interest of entrepreneurs created the prosperity of the United States.

Corruption of the Commerce Clause has turned the Unites States from the principles that Adam Smith discussed. The corruption has resulted in a takeover of the U.S. economy by the regulatory state. In the regulatory state, central planners set the standards. They decide what is best. They ban products such as certain drugs, raw milk, and one hundred watt incandescent light bulbs.

Before the government and insurance company takeover of health care, the medical standards were set by individual physicians. They would go to meetings and listen to papers by the experts. They would discuss with their peers what they thought of the various experts and how to best treat diseases. The individuals would then treat their patients based on their best knowledge. This produced a bottoms up standard of health care.

Today, we have "clinical practice guidelines." These are guidelines or standards that are dictated to the practicing physicians from above. To get paid by insurance companies, physicians must follow them. These are the standards of central planners, not the standards of what individual physicians believe is the best treatment for their patients. This is producing a top down standard of health care.

Corruption of the Commerce Clause has resulted in over 150 regulatory agencies such as the Food and Drug Administration (FDA), the Environmental Protection Agency (EPA), and the

Occupational Safety and Health Administration (OSHA).

Many of these agencies are run by people unofficially known as czars. Here is a small sampling from 2012:

- AIDS Czar – Jeffrey Crowley
- Car Czar – Ron Bloom,
- Climate Czar – Todd Stern,
- Domestic Violence Czar – Lynn Rosenthal
- And so forth

Before the regulatory state, Congress would make a law and the executive branch would enforce the law. If a person violated the law, they could take their case to a jury trial in the federal courts.

It is different in the regulatory state. Regulatory agencies have the power to create a regulation and then the same regulatory agency can charge a person with violating the regulation they made. This goes against good government where one body makes the law and another enforces the law.

Even worse, some regulatory agencies have the unconstitutional power to have appeals to their rules tried at the same regulatory agency. Often the regulatory agency will fine the accused for each day they do not comply. This can be a significant expense and the fines accumulate while the case is under appeal. This is a deterrent for the accused to challenge the agency's rules. These regulatory agency rules comes with heavy fines and jail time. Any law that has the penalty of jail should be a criminal case and the accused should have a right to a jury trial.

The Sixth Amendment

In all criminal prosecutions, the accused shall enjoy the right to a speedy and public trial, by an impartial jury..."

Chapter 5
CORRUPTION - OATH OF OFFICE

Article II, Clause 6
Oath of Office of the President
"I do solemnly swear (or affirm) that I will faithfully execute the Office of President of the United States, and will to the best of my Ability, preserve, protect and defend the Constitution of the United States."

Article VI, Clause 3
Oath of Office of
All federal, state, and local officials
The Senators and Representatives before mentioned, and the Members of the several State Legislatures, and all executive and judicial Officers, both of the United States and of the several States, shall be bound by Oath or Affirmation, to support this Constitution;

Our elected officials pledge to support the Constitution and it says that the laws of the United States are the supreme law of the land when the laws are pursuant to the Constitution.

Supremacy Clause
Article 6, Clause 2
This Constitution, and the laws of the United States which shall be made in pursuance thereof; and all treaties made, or which shall be made, under the authority of

the United States, shall be the supreme law of the land

The Constitution does not say that the Supreme Court is the sole judge of whether a law or regulation is pursuant to the Constitution. The Tenth Amendment reads:

The powers not delegated to the United States by the Constitution, nor prohibited by it to the States, are reserved to the States respectively, or to the people.

The Tenth Amendment says that where the Constitution is silent, the power is reserved to the states. Therefore, it is not constitutional for the Supreme Court to rule that it has the sole power to judge if a law is pursuant to the Constitution. State and local officials are also required by their oath of office to support the Constitution.

They support the Constitution by enforcing constitutional federal laws and by deeming laws not pursuant to the Constitution to be null and void and not to be enforced. They are bound by their oath of office to do this.

When asked about this, some politicians have said that it is up to the Supreme Court to decide the constitutionality of federal laws. They are corrupted when they say this because they are duty bound to support the Constitution, not the Supreme Court's interpretation of what it says. The oath of office should be a campaign issue for every elected office in the United States.

Chapter 6
RESISTANCE TO
COMMERCE CLAUSE CORRUPTION
Corruption is a deviation from the ideal

Resistance to corruption of the commerce clause can occur in many different ways.

Individuals

It starts with individuals becoming informed about the many problems that results from a powerful centralized government verses a federation. Once educated the individual can become part of the resistance.

An effective way to educate people is to discover a cause of theirs where there is a conflict between federal and state laws. This could be something such as mothers who believe that raw milk helps their children overcome some medical problems like colic and allergies. Once you find a cause with conflict, explain how our federation is set up for states to make the laws rather than the federal government. You can then point out that nullification by the state is one way of eliminating these conflicting federal laws.

Another way for Individuals to work for nullification is by making appointments to discuss their concerns with their public officials. Always be respectful. Make sure they know how you feel about your issue and then listen attentively as they tell you how they feel about it. Another good point is to tell them that you have more confidence in the laws they would create, than those of the federal government.

You might give them a copy of the U.S. Constitution and remind them that they took an oath to support it when federal laws are pursuant to the Constitution. If the law is unconstitutional, then you believe they are duty bound to nullify it. The oath is found at Article VI, Clause 3:

This Constitution, and the Laws of the United States which shall be made in Pursuance thereof ... shall be the supreme Law of the Land;

Do not expect them to change their position at this time but you have planted, or helped nurture, the seed.

Individuals can also be effective at forums attended by government officials. They can bring up the nullification and interposition issues. Remember, your real purpose is to educate the group about the issue, not to embarrass the official. As always, it is good to personalize an issue of conflict between the federal government and other levels of government such the banning of one hundred watt incandescent light bulbs.

Many Individual are members of groups. It is through these organizations that similar, but perhaps even more effective, lobbying can be done.

Groups

It is normal for people with causes and, commercial interests to join groups with similar interests. If you are a member of such a group, then bring up nullification at meetings with these groups.

State Medical Societies have a formal process for doing this. Below are some pertinent parts of such a resolution from the Indiana State Medical Association:

Whereas, one of the primary roles of physicians is to relieve pain and suffering as much as possible; and

Whereas, to achieve this end, physicians have always been willing to use potent, potentially harmful, even potentially lethal drugs (such as morphine); and

...

RESOLVED, that the Indiana State Medical Association join the American college of Physicians (ACP) and the Institute of Medicine (IOM) in encouraging legislation that would allow licensed physicians to legally prescribe medical marijuana to patients suffering medical conditions where, in their medical judgment, it is the best therapeutic option for the patient; and be it further

RESOLVED, that the ISMA encourage state legislation that would provide a mechanism for the production and distribution of marijuana for medical purposes, and provide the legal means, such as medical necessity defense, to thwart the federal government from interfering with this effort.

The last sentence brings up the important point that if this is passed, there will be a conflict with federal law. They acknowledge that the federal government could prosecute a citizen for growing, distributing or using marijuana. They suggest that the state of Indiana provide a means of defense for individuals who might be charged with violation of federal law but not state law.

The purpose of your going to the meeting is to educate the group about how nullification can advance their cause. If they agree, your next purpose is to have the group agree to write a letter to government officials about your concerns and what you would like the officials to do about it.

Letter of Protest

When a state or local legislator finds that a federal law is unconstitutional, they can introduce legislation to have an official letter sent to federal officials. The letter would explain their complaint, such as SB 1178 from Arizona:

44-7801. State goods and services not subject to congressional authority under commerce clause power

A. ALL GOODS GROWN, MANUFACTURED OR MADE IN THIS STATE AND ALL SERVICES PERFORMED IN THIS STATE WHEN THE GOODS OR SERVICES ARE SOLD, MAINTAINED OR RETAINED IN THIS STATE ARE NOT SUBJECT TO THE AUTHORITY OF CONGRESS UNDER ITS CONSTITUTIONAL POWER TO REGULATE COMMERCE AMONG

THE SEVERAL STATES.

The letter would ask the federal government to repeal the offending law or regulation. It would specify to which federal officials it should be sent, such as this one from Utah:

BE IT FURTHER RESOLVED that a copy of this resolution should be sent to the Majority Leader of the United States Senate, the Speaker of the United States House of Representatives, to the Justices of the Supreme Court, and to the members of Utah's congressional delegation.

These protest letters are not nullification by the states. It does give notice to the federal government that the states believe the offending law or regulation is unconstitutional.

The letters could also contain a threat. If the federal government does not repeal the unconstitutional law then the state officials will introduce legislation to nullify it.

Legislation - Nullification Alone
A Dangerous Business

Although many disagree with marijuana use, it is instructive to study the medical legalization conflict between federal and state law. It could just as well have been about raw milk. In 1992, California legalized medical marijuana. With legalization, came with many regulations and restrictions.

Their marijuana laws do not address the conflict with federal laws. They do not say that the federal anti marijuana laws are unconstitutional. This is especially pertinent since the federal government unconstitutionally bans marijuana, so how could they regulate the trade of what they ban?

Matthew Davies has a masters degree in business. He entered the medical marijuana business in 2009 and grew it into an eight million dollar business that was legal in California. Before this, he obtained legal advice and followed all the state laws.

In 2012, U.S. attorney, Benjamin Wagner, an Obama appointee, charged Davies with breaking federal law and wanted a fifteen year jail sentence. Mr. Davies is in the process of a plea bargain with a five year jail sentence.

Matthew Davies and family

Mr. Davies is the father of two young children. He says he would have entered another business if he had known that there was this type of danger from conflicting federal and state laws.

The U.S. Congress, President, and the Supreme Court take an oath to uphold the constitution. They are corrupt when they make and enforce anti marijuana laws that are not under the powers authorized by the Constitution.

California politicians created a law that legalizes medical marijuana and conflicts with U.S. laws. The California politicians took an oath to support the U.S. Constitution. They are corrupt if they made this law while believing that the federal anti-marijuana laws were constitutional.

What California should do is create legislation that explains that Article I, Section 3, Paragraph 8 enumerates the seventeen powers of Congress and that banning marijuana is not one of these powers. They should say that they do not agree with the Supreme Court ruling in Filburn v. Wickard. Mr. Davies is only legally selling his product in California and not across state lines. They should develop language about how they would protect California citizens from the federal government trying to enforce unconstitutional laws. Because the California legislators failed to do this, Mr. Davies faces federal prosecutors without help from the state of California.

In 2012, Washington State passed Initiative 502 that legalizes the recreational use of marijuana. Below is Part I that explains the intent of the act:

"PART I. The people intend to stop treating adult marijuana use as a crime and try a new approach that:
(1) Allows law enforcement resources to be focused on violent and property crimes;
(2) Generates new state and local tax revenue

*for education, health care, research, and
substance abuse prevention; and
(3) Takes marijuana out of the hands of illegal
drug organizations and brings it under a tightly
regulated, state-licensed system ... This
measure authorizes the state liquor control
board to regulate and tax marijuana for
persons twenty-one years of age and older,
and add a new threshold for driving under the
influence of marijuana..."*

As with California, the politicians of Washington State are morally corrupted. They made no provisions to protect their citizens from the federal government prosecuting them for federal laws that are not pursuant to the U.S. Constitution.

There is serious talk of the federal government making some changes to the federal anti-marijuana laws to allow some personal possession. This would show how nullification efforts often precede changes in unconstitutional federal laws.

Intrastate Commerce Act
Goods that are made and sold in a state
are not subject to federal regulations.

Regulatory agencies usually gain their Constitutional authority by way of the Commerce Clause. As previously discussed, in Wickard v Filburn (1942), the Supreme Court ruled that federal regulation of producing almost anything was constitutional because all goods are part of commerce even when not for sale. This is because the Supreme Court said that making something for your own use means that you would not buy it on the open market and this would affect commerce among the states. This ruling went against the original intent of the Commerce Clause.

Most regulatory agencies were created by the lobbying efforts of various factions. For instance, the Occupational Safety and Health Administration (OSHA) was created by factions that wanted to assure that workers were safe. The federal government has a hard time trying to make regulations for coal minors in West Virginia, farmers in the mid west, the carpet industry in Georgia, and so forth. This could have been done better at the state level where they have a better knowledge of their local industries.

OSHA causes great expense for business, which has caused many small businesses to shut down. It is usually easier for big businesses to follow regulations because of the economy of scale. Blacksmithing can be a dangerous business. There can be eye injuries, smoke inhalation can cause significant problems, the shops can be fire hazards, etc. Recently OSHA has been accelerating their regulations on blacksmith shops. Some of these new regulations require expensive changes causing many blacksmith shops to shut down.

The Food and Drug Administration (FDA) has expanded its scope from regulating safety to regulating efficacy. This determines whether the drug is useful for a specific disease. Interestingly, once a drug gets on the market, it is often found to have other uses and unexpected complications. Federal regulators are like the rest of us. They cannot predict the future.

In this environment, it is expensive and time consuming to get a drug approved. The delay in approval often denies patients obtaining life saving drugs. The increased cost of approval increases the cost for patients.

Congress created the Environmental Protection Agency (EPA) to limit pollutants. It is assumed that constitutional authority comes by way of the Commerce Clause because it allows regulation of industries, and they pollute. This gives them authority to develop rules and regulations under the Clean Air Act. Recently the EPA said that water was a pollutant because in storms it stirred up sediment. It told officials in Fairfax County, VA that they had to cut the storm water drainage by one half. The county sued and with the help of VA Attorney General Ken Cuccinelli, they won the case in federal courts. Going to the courts when these agencies flex their regulatory muscles is an iffy and expensive proposition.

Cuccinelli has written a book called, *The Last Line of Defense: The New Fight for American Liberty.* It is due to come out on February 12, 2013. He makes the case that state attorneys general are the last line of defense by suing to reverse unconstitutional law and regulations in the federal courts.

However, using the Court system to nullify unconstitutional federal laws is time consuming and expensive. The Nullification Manifesto makes the case that nullification and interposition is the true last line of defense.

Another way is for Fairfax County to nullify the agency's rulings by declaring them not pursuant to the Constitution and therefore null and void and not to be followed. It would seem it would be quite difficult for the EPA to force Fairfax County to cut its storm runoff in half without the help of state and local governments.

States can resist corruption of the Commerce Clause by passing laws that nullify federal laws regulating commerce within their states. They should also make provisions to protect their citizens from federal agents.

In 2012, Florida introduced HB 553 to be cited as "Intrastate Commerce Act." It has both nullification and interposition in the bill. Below is some of the language:

WHEREAS, the Tenth Amendment to the Constitution of the United States holds that the Federal Government may exercise only the powers that have been delegated to it in the constitution, and

WHEREAS, the Ninth Amendment to the Constitution of the United States guarantees to the people rights not enumerated in the constitution and reserves to the people of this state those rights, and

WHEREAS, article I, section 8, clause 3 of the Constitution of the United States empowers the

Federal Government to regulate commerce among the several states, and ...

(2) Goods that are grown, manufactured, or made in this state and that are sold, maintained, or retained in this state, and services that are performed in this state, are not subject to the authority of the Congress of the United States under its constitutional power to regulate commerce among the several states.

(3) Any official, agent, or employee of the Federal Government or any employee of an entity providing services to the Federal Government who attempts to enforce any federal law, rule, or regulation in violation of this section commits a felony of the third degree, punishable as provided in s. 775.082, s. 775.083, or s. 775.084, Florida Statutes.

This legislation died in committee but it is probably a matter of time until such acts become state law.

Chapter 7
THE WARRANT

Fourth Amendment

The right of the people to be secure in their persons, houses, papers, and effects, against unreasonable searches and seizures, shall not be violated, and no Warrants shall issue, but upon probable cause, supported by Oath or affirmation, and particularly describing the place to be searched, and the persons or things to be seized.

A warrant is issued by a judge or magistrate, which permits an otherwise illegal act that would violate individual rights such as privacy. It gives the person executing the warrant protection from damages. Both the federal government and the states require warrants before performing searches.

Individuals often have a federal agent demanding that they comply with a law or regulation. To comply is often very expensive and complying might prevent them from using their property as they desired.

If this happens, the individual should determine if they think the demand by the federal agent is constitutional. If they believe it is an unconstitutional demand, they should start by discussing this with their sheriff.

The county sheriff is a very important officer of the peace. He, like other public officials, is required to take an oath of office to support the U.S. Constitution. If public officials uphold their oath, then it is their duty to declare a federal law not pursuant to the Constitution as null and void and not to be followed.

The county sheriff is the only officer of the peace who is elected to office. For the sheriff to nullify a law does not require the action of any other governmental agency. Nullification and use of warrants can become an important election issue for sheriffs.

A constitutional sheriff will know that a federal agent needs a warrant before entering your property to inspect it. The warrant is a powerful tool in the nullification movement. If he is a constitutional sheriff, he should be able to help protect you from unconstitutional demands. If he is not, you should work to elect a constitutional sheriff to take his place.

Here is an example of how this has worked in the past. David Hochstetler of Elkhart County, Indiana, is an Amish dairy farmer who produces raw milk. The FDA unconstitutionally regulates raw milk using the commerce clause as justification. Federal FDA agents visited Hochstetler's farm a few times without a search warrant.

In 2011, a federal prosecutor issued a subpoena for Hochstetler to appear in federal court in Detroit, Michigan. Hoshestler went to his county Sheriff, Brad Rogers for help. The sheriff said to Mr. Hochstetler, "I will protect you in Elkhart County. I can't protect you in Detroit ... Are you ready for some sparks to fly?" Hochstetler said he was.

Sheriff Rogers then wrote a letter to the federal prosecutor, "Any further attempts to inspect this farm without a warrant signed by a local judge, based on probable cause, will result in Federal inspectors' removal or arrest for trespassing by my officers or I." A few days later, Mr. Hochstetler received a certified letter that the Department of Justice had withdrawn the subpoena.

A federal agent is like any other government official. If not invited, they need a warrant to enter your property. If they do not obtain this, they are trespassing.

In 2007, Mike and Chantell Sackett bought two-thirds of an acre of lakefront property in Idaho for $25,000 to build their dream home. They started filling in some low spots when the EPA stepped in and said they had filled in a wetland. This was because it had standing water on it during part of the year. They were told they must comply or face fines of up to $75,000 a day and they were told there was no sensible way to appeal. The Pacific Legal Foundation stepped in and helped. They took it all the way to the Supreme Court where the Sacketts won.

It took them five years along with significant aggravation and money to reverse the ruling. Most of the time, people just give up.

Early on the Sacketts might have gone to their sheriff. If he was a constitutional sheriff, he might have required the EPA agent to get a warrant from a local judge. If the judge refused, the EPA agent would not have been able to inspect the property.

If a federal agent asks for a warrant in trying to enforce a constitutional federal law, then of course the local judge should give him the warrant.

Another way would be for the Sacketts to try to obtain help from their state government through nullification and interposition. For instance, Indiana Senator Dennis Kruse introduced Indiana Bill 0127 in 2013. If enacted, this could effectively nullify much of the regulatory state:

> *Arrests and searches by federal employees. Provides that a federal employee who is not designated by state law to act as a state law enforcement officer may not make an arrest, a search, or a seizure in Indiana without the written permission of the sheriff or the designee of the sheriff who has jurisdiction in the county in which the arrest, search, or seizure will occur. Provides certain exceptions. Provides that if an arrest, a search, or a seizure is made without the sheriff's written permission, the federal employee must be prosecuted under Indiana law and charged with an offense appropriate to the circumstances. Provides that under the Tenth Amendment of the Constitution of the United States and Indiana's compact with the other states, the general assembly declares that any federal law that purports to provide federal employees with the authority of a sheriff in Indiana is not recognized by and is specifically rejected by the state of Indiana and is invalid in Indiana.*

Many of these types of bills can be found at TenthAmendmentCenter.com under "Legislative tracking."

Chapter 8
JURY NULLIFICATION

Sixth Amendment

In all criminal prosecutions, the accused shall enjoy the right to a speedy and public trial, by an impartial jury..."

One reason for a jury trial is to give the accused the defense that the law or regulation he is accused of violating is unjust or unconstitutional. When the jury acquits because of this, it is called jury nullification. This has a long history dating back to English common law. In the United States it was widespread during prohibition when almost sixty percent of the prosecutions against alcohol use were nullified. This nullification by juries was a major reason for the repeal of Prohibition Amendment.

Jurors cannot be prosecuted for jury nullification.

In United States v. Dougherty, 1972, a lower federal court ruled that a jury had the right to nullify but the judge did not have to inform juries about this. Jurors can be struck from the jury if they say they believe in jury nullification.

Because of the above, jury nullification is seldom practiced today. In most cases, judges rule that defense lawyers are not permitted to bring up jury nullification as a defense or even mention it. A commonly given reason why defense lawyers cannot use the defense of jury nullification is because they take an oath to uphold the law. The U.S. Constitution says they must also take an oath to support the U.S. Constitution. The Constitution says that only those laws that are constitutional are the **"supreme law of the land"** If a defense lawyer believes his client is accused of an unconstitutional law then he has every right to use this defense.

Dr. Stanislaw Burzynski is a physician who founded the controversial Burzynski Research Institute Inc. It uses an alternative cancer treatment. The safety of the drug is known but it is not clear if it works, and for this reason was not approved as a cancer treatment by the U.S. Food and Drug Administration (FDA). The FDA charged him with using an unapproved treatment and brought him before five grand juries and a jury trial that resulted in a hung jury.

He has had complaints from the Texas Board of Medical examiners. He has some enthusiastic supporters, some who were members of the federal grand jury that refused to indict him. It is likely that the hung jury was a jury nullification.

Resistance

The more people who are informed about jury nullification, the more effective it will be. There have been some recent TV shows that explore the issue. Some groups have been handing out fliers to jurors at court houses, and that has led to arrests. Eighty year old Julian Heicklen was charged with handing out literature concerning jury nullification.   He was acquitted in 2012. Federal Judge, Kimba M. Wood wrote that he did not violate the jury tampering statute because he was not trying to influence a specific case.

In the case of the marijuana grower, Matthew Davies, it is interesting to speculate how it might have gone if his lawyer had used the defense of jury nullification. It is likely that at least one of the California jurors would have voted not guilty because the federal law was unjust and unconstitutional.

State Representative Charles Gregory of Georgia has introduced HB 25, Fully Informed Jury Act of 2013. It says:

> In a criminal jury trial, the court shall permit the defendant or his or her counsel to argue for jury nullification in its role as the judges of the law and the facts pursuant to Article I, Section I, Paragraph XI of the Constitution.

Chapter 9
CORRUPTION - BILL OF RIGHTS
Corruption is a deviation from the ideal

The Bill of Rights are the first ten amendments to the U.S. Constitution. These amendments were to assure that the federal government would not make laws that infringe upon some of the basic unalienable rights that Jefferson wrote about in the Declaration of Independence. The federal government has corrupted the Bill of Rights in two ways.

The first is legislative corruption. This occurs with federal laws such as The Gun Control Act (GCA) of 1968. This Act prohibits the selling of firearms to certain classes of people. This corrupts the Second Amendment's right to bear arms.

The second is judicial corruption. This occurs when a federal court rules that a state, county, or city is violating one of the amendments of the Bill of Rights. This is called the incorporation doctrine. An example would be when federal courts dictate to a lower level of government that it cannot place the Ten Commandments on a court house wall. It reasoned that by doing this, it is establishing a religion and this violates the First Amendment.

The original intention of the Bill of Rights was to apply only to the federal government. It was not to apply to the states. This was confirmed in 1833 with Barron v. Baltimore where the Supreme Court ruled that the Fifth Amendment did not apply to the states.

To understand how The Supreme Court incorporated The Bill of Rights to the states we must first understand the purpose of The Fourteenth Amendment that reads in Section 1:

No State shall make or enforce any law which shall abridge the privileges or immunities of citizens of the United States; nor shall any State deprive any person of life, liberty, or property, without due process of law; nor deny to any person within its jurisdiction the equal protection of the laws

This was ratified after the Civil War to assure that state laws did not discriminate against the recently freed slaves. Initially, this failed because of the "Separate But Equal" doctrine of Jim Crow. The civil rights movement of the 1950s and 60s mercifully ended this practice.

In 1876, the Supreme Court in The United States v, Cruikshank reaffirmed that the Bill of Rights did not apply to the states. They reversed this in 1925 with Gitlow v. New York. Benjamin Gitlow. The Supreme Court ruled that the First Amendment rights of freedom of speech and of the press were:

*Among the fundamental personal rights and liberties enumerated in the Bill of Rights and protected by the **due process** clause of the Fourteenth Amendment from impairment by the states.*

Since then, the Supreme Court has incorporated many of the amendments of the Bill of Rights to the states. The next sections discuss the legislative and judicial corruption of the First, Second, and Fourth Amendments.

First Amendment
Congress shall make no law respecting an establishment of religion, or prohibiting the free exercise thereof; or abridging the freedom of speech, or of the press...

Legislative corruption of the First Amendment occurs with campaign finance reform. This was done to limit the power of the special interest groups or factions. As discussed in Chapter 2, James Madison was also concerned about factions. He said they were, "The mortal disease under which popular governments everywhere have perished." Madison would control them with a federation where the central government had limited powers. He said. "The influence of factious leaders may kindle a flame within their particular States, but will be unable to spread a general conflagration through the other States."

Corruption of the Commerce Clause has allowed the federal government to take over the economy through regulatory agencies. These agencies are controlled by factions. To combat this, Congress legislated campaign reform beginning in 1972 with The Federal Election Campaign Act (FECA) of 1972. This required candidates to disclose sources of campaign contributions and expenditures. In 1974, they put limits on contributions and created another federal agency, the Federal Election Commission (FEC).

To get elected to office is often expensive because candidates must get their message out through paid advertising. Limiting the money going to advertising limits the freedom of speech. However, money is still going into politics. Influential donors of 2012 included: ActBlue - a liberal policy organization, Goldman Sachs - Securities and investments, AT&T - Telecom Services, Citigroup - Finance & insurance, National Association or Realtors, Trade Unions, Public Sector Unions, General Electric, American Bankers Association, Lockheed Martin-Defense, Pfizer - Pharmaceuticals, National Education Association, Google, Walmart, Microsoft, Blue Cross Blue Shield - health insurance, etc. Campaign finance does not work. The factions are still in control.

Judicial corruption occurs when the Supreme Court dictates that religious displays in public buildings is the establishment of a religion. In McCreary County, Ky., v. ACLU 2005, The Supreme Court ruled that displaying the Ten Commandments on a Kentucky Court House favored monotheistic religion and had to be removed by way of the Fourteenth Amendment.

The Court felt that McCreary County had done this on purely religious grounds. The Supreme Court ruled that government agencies may display the Ten Commandments as long as it is for historical reasons along with historical secular documents such as the Bill of Rights.

The Supreme Court also ruled that McCreary County must pay $250,000 to the ACLU for their lawyer fees.

Second Amendment

"A well regulated Militia, being necessary to the security of a free State, the right of the people to keep and bear Arms, shall not be infringed."

Legislative corruption The of 1968 is of the Second Amendment. It prohibits the selling of firearms to certain classes of people such as unlawful user of, or addicted to, any controlled substance. This infringes on the right of some people to buy firearms. The states have the power to do this. The federal government does not.

Following the tragic Newtown Connecticut school shooting in 2012, President Obama signed 23 executive orders on guns. One of these was:

4. Direct the Attorney General to review categories of individuals prohibited from having a gun to make sure dangerous people are not slipping through the cracks.

In response to this infringement on the right to bear arms, many state lawmakers have introduced nullification laws.

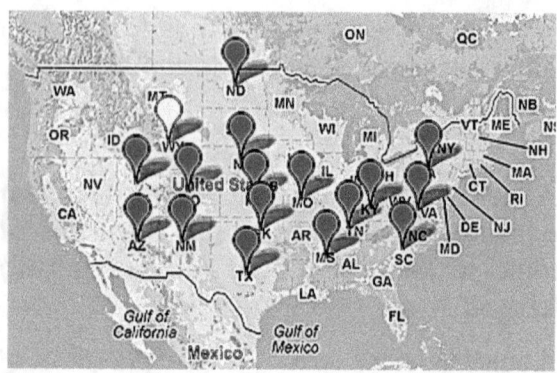

The pins represent nullification legislations compiled by the TenthAmendmentCenter.com

Wyoming's House Bill, NO. HB0104 is such a law has already passed both houses. It nullifies any federal law that tries to limit the size of firearm magazines or firearms.

1. AN ACT relating to firearms; providing that any federal law
2 which attempts to ban a semi-automatic firearm or to limit
3 the size of a magazine of a firearm or other limitation on
4 firearms in this state shall be unenforceable in Wyoming;

It brings in the corruption of the Commerce Clause by saying if a gun is made and sold in Wyoming, federal laws do not apply:

9 ...a personal firearm, a firearm
10 accessory or ammunition that is owned or

manufactured
11 commercially or privately in Wyoming and that remains
12 exclusively within the borders of Wyoming...

The next part says that federal agents are guilty of a crime if they violate the individual rights of privacy. This act has significant penalties for U.S. agents who violate a Wyoming citizen's right to privacy.

...shall be guilty of a misdemeanor felony and, upon conviction, shall be subject to imprisonment for not more less than one (1) year and one (1) day or more than five (5) years, a fine of not more than two thousand dollars ($2,000.00) five thousand dollars ($5,000.00), or both.

If a Wyoming citizen is prosecuted for breaking a federal antigun law, the act gives the Wyoming attorney general the ability to defend the accused.

(c) The attorney general may defend a citizen of Wyoming who is prosecuted by the United States government for violation of a federal law relating to the manufacture, sale, transfer or possession of a firearm, a firearm accessory or ammunition owned or manufactured and retained exclusively within the borders of Wyoming.

Judicial corruption of the Second Amendment by the Supreme Court occurred in 2010 with McDonald v. Chicago. With this, The Court nullified Chicago's ban on handguns by ruling that the right to **"keep and bear arms"** was incorporated against the states by way of the Fourteenth Amendment. They went on to say that certain firearms restrictions mentioned in District of Columbia v. Heller are assumed permissible and not directly dealt with in this case.

Most states have some gun laws, such as keeping them out of the hands of convicted felons and the mentally ill. This book takes no stand on the wisdom of such state regulations. It was the total ban in Chicago that caused the Supreme Court to nullify the Chicago gun laws. Since then, Chicago has changed their laws so as not to totally ban guns. It is contradictory that, "Shall not be infringed" can apply to a total ban on guns but not antigun regulations.

At this time, the majority of the pro-gun and antigun groups approve of the Second Amendment being incorporated to the states. A reason the antigun groups approve is that most of them agree with the centralization of power. They know they already have federal antigun laws on the books such as Gun Control Act and the Brady Bill. This allows for federal government back ground check on some hand gun purchases. The antigun group will continue to work for gun control at both the state and federal level.

Amendment IV

The right of the people to be secure in their persons, houses, papers, and effects, against unreasonable searches and seizures, shall not be violated, and no Warrants shall issue, but upon probable cause, supported by Oath or affirmation, and particularly describing the place to be searched, and the persons or things to be seized.

Legislative corruption of the Fourth Amendment to privacy occurs when the IRS requests access to all of our personal financial transactions. This initial request is not covered by the Fourth Amendment because it not a criminal case. It is about paying your taxes and does not require a warrant. If you refuse to comply, the IRS agent issues a summons to produce records. If you refuse the summons, Section 7604 of the IRS codes allows the agent to arrest you and you can by punished for contempt.

Incongruously, the initial civil request for records can end up with imprisonment for the citizen. By doing this, the federal government by way of the IRS nullifies the Fourth Amendment rights to privacy, the Fifth Amendment right against self incrimination, and the Sixth Amendment right to a trial by jury.

This corruption could be nullified by state governments creating legislations to assure that the federal government affords the citizens of its state, the protections afforded in the Bill of Rights. They could then say that all requests for records by the IRS require warrants describing the probable cause, supported by Oath or affirmation, and particularly describing the place to be searched, and the persons or things to be seized.

Judicial corruption of the Fourth Amendment occurred in Roe v. Wade. This ruling incorporated the Fourth Amendment of privacy to the states. The Supreme Court ruled that state laws prohibiting abortions violated the Fourth Amendment. With incorporation, a woman's right to privacy was protected from federal and state laws.

Discussion

For Conservatives, there is a disconnect between the incorporation of the Second and Fourth Amendments against the states. On one hand, most conservatives are pleased with the result of incorporation of the Second Amendment. Their hope is that no level of government could create antigun laws. However, in actuality, there are antigun laws on the books at both the federal and state governments. On the other hand, most conservatives are displeased with incorporation of the Fourth Amendment against the states because this nullified state antiabortion laws.

An ancient Chinese proverb goes, "No One Rules If No One Obeys." The incorporation doctrine may be applicable to this. With incorporation, there is no federal law to nullify. There is only the Supreme Court, ruling that it has the power to nullify state laws that violated the federal Bill of Rights. The Supreme Court must rely on other levels of government to implement its rulings. The states can nullify their ruling by saying the Supreme Court does not have the Constitutional power to incorporate the Bill of Rights against them. They would ignore the federal courts rulings. Since the states are not nullifying a federal law, there would be less incentive for other levels to become involved in trying to enforce the federal courts rulings.

For instance, in McCreary County v. ACLU, the Supreme Court ruled that they could not hang a picture of the Ten Commandments in their public buildings. They also ruled that the county must pay ACLU $250,000. What would happen if McCreary County nullified the ruling by disobeying it? Most likely, the McCreary County sheriff and the State of Kentucky would not enforce the ruling. This leaves only the executive branch of the federal government to enforce the ruling. As of 2013, McReary County has not paid the $250,000 to the ACLU.

The same thing would apply to Chicago and their ban on guns. If Chicago refused to obey the ruling, it is unlikely that the state of Illinois would enforce the ruling. It would be quite amusing to see President Obama sending the federal government in to make sure the citizens of Chicago could bear arms.

Tenth Amendment
The powers not delegated to the United States by the Constitution, nor prohibited by it to the States, are reserved to the States respectively, or to the people.

Congress can constitutionally only make laws using the seventeen powers in Article I, Section 8, or the Constitution. The Tenth Amendment echoes this. Congress, the President, and the Supreme Court are corrupt when they create and legitimize laws and federal agencies not pursuant to the Constitution. Federal agents are corrupt when they enforce these unconstitutional laws and regulations.

Resistance

States, counties, sheriffs, cities, and the people, using the Tenth Amendment, can declare unconstitutional federal laws to be null and void and not to be followed. When challenged with law suits, they should not participate in the federal courts. If this happened, the size of the federal government would drastically shrink.

Chapter 10
CORRUPTION - HABEAS CORPUS
Corruption is a deviation from the ideal

Article I, Section 9, Clause 2
The Privilege of the Writ of Habeas Corpus shall not be suspended, unless when in Cases of Rebellion or Invasion the public Safety may require it.

The National Defense Authorization Act of 2012 (NDAA) is an anti terrorist act that authorizes the President to jail American citizens indefinitely without bringing the accused into court and accusing them of a crime. This violates habeas corpus which says that the accused must be brought before a judge or jury to prevent unlawful detention.

There are multiple state and local legislations about this. S. 92, 2103, says that the state of Carolina will not cooperate with the federal government in trying to enforce this unconstitutional law:

The enactment into law by the United States Congress of Section 1021 and 1022 of the National Defense Authorization Act of 2012, P.L 112-81, is a direct threat to the liberty, security, and well being of the people of South Carolina, and was adopted by the United States Congress in violation of the limits of federal power provided in the United States Constitution.

Section 8-1-15. No agency of the State, agency

of a political subdivision of the State, officer or employee of the State, officer or employee of a political subdivision of the State, acting in his official capacity, to include any member of the South Carolina Military Department on official duty, or employees of any state or local detention facility may engage in any activity that aids an agency of the armed forces of the United States in execution of 50 U.S.C. 1541, as provided by the National Defense Authorization Act for Fiscal Year 2012, in the investigation, prosecution, or detainment of any citizen of the United States in violation of Section 3, Article I, and Section 14, Article I of the South Carolina Constitution.

Chapter 11
CORRUPTION - HEALTH CARE
Corruption is a deviation from the ideal

The Patient Protection and Affordable Care Act (PPACA), commonly called ObamaCare, is 2400 pages long and has generated at least 13,000 pages of regulations and still counting. Twenty-six states participated in a law suit to declare ObamaCare unconstitutional. It was ruled constitutional. Supreme Court Chief Justice John Roberts wrote the majority opinion. He said ObamaCare was not constitutional using the Commerce Clause but it was constitutional because it was a de facto tax. They also ruled that the states did not have to participate in the expansion of Medicaid. If they did not participate, the Supreme Court ruled the federal government could not withhold current Medicaid payments to states.

Many states are making laws to nullify much of ObamaCare using the argument that administering the nation's medical care is not one of the powers given to Congress in the Constitution. Assemblywoman Alison McHose of New Jersey did not agree that ruling ObamaCare a tax made it constitutional. In 2013, she introduced Bill No. 861. It nullifies the Patient Protection and Affordable Care Act or ObamaCare. It has elements of nullification, non cooperation, and interposition.

Nullification

1.   The Legislature finds and declares that:

a.   The people of the several states comprising the United States of America created the federal government to be their agent for certain enumerated purposes, and nothing more;

b.   Amendment X to the United States Constitution defines the total scope of federal power as being that which has been delegated by the people of the several states to the federal government, and all power not delegated to the federal government in the Constitution of the United States is reserved to the states respectively, or to the people themselves;

c.   The assumption of power that the federal government has made by enacting the "Patient Protection and Affordable Care Act" interferes with the right of the people of the State of New Jersey to regulate health care as they see fit, and makes a mockery of James Madison's assurance in Number 45 of the Federalist Papers that the "powers delegated" to the federal government are "few and defined," while those of the states are "numerous and indefinite"; and

d.   The federal act is not authorized by the Constitution of the United States and violates its true meaning and intent as given by its founders and ratifiers, and is hereby declared to be invalid in this State, to not be recognized by this State, to be specifically rejected by this State, and to be considered null and void and of no force and effect in this State.

Non Cooperation

2. d.   Any public officer or employee of this State who seeks to enforce an act, order, law, statute, rule, or regulation of the United States government in violation of this act shall be guilty of a disorderly persons offense and, notwithstanding the provisions of N.J.S.2C:43-3 to the contrary, for every such offense shall be fined not less than $500 nor more than $1,000, or be imprisoned for a term of not more than two years, or both, in the discretion of the court.

Interposition

c. Any official, agent, or employee of the United States government or any employee of a corporation, firm, or other entity providing services to the United States government who seeks to enforce an act, order, law, statute, rule, or regulation of the government of the United States in violation of this act shall be guilty of a crime of the third degree and, notwithstanding the provisions of N.J.S.2C: 43-3 to the contrary, for every such offense shall be fined not less than $1,000 nor more than $5,000, or be imprisoned for a term of not more than five years, or both, in the discretion of the court.

All elected state officials take an oath to uphold the U.S. Constitution. Assemblywoman Alison McHose is a constitutional Representative who is upholding her oath. She has found that a federal law is not pursuant to the Constitution and has introduced legislation to nullify it.

At the time of this writing, this legislation had not come to a vote.

The Problem

The problem with nullifying ObamaCare is that the United States has a dysfunctional health care system.

The ideal would be to go back to what we had before World War II, where people bought most of their medical care out-of-pocket like almost everything else. If there was a big bill, some would borrow and others might have catastrophic insurance. Hospitals had wards for the indigent. Doctors charged less money for the poor and did charity work. States, counties, and cities, helped subsidize the health care primarily in city-county public hospitals.

This system started to change during World War II. The government, in its wisdom, started allowing employers to take some of a worker's salary and use it to pay for tax-free medical insurance. Most workers were happy with this. However, there were problems, such as many workers losing their medical care when they changed jobs or retired. Consider that before 1913, this could not have happened because there was no Sixteenth Amendment to our Constitution and thus no income tax to encourage job-based medical insurance.

Another problem with the income tax was that it discouraged savings. This is why IRAs are so popular. They spare savings from the income tax. Savings were also discouraged in 1913 with the establishment of the Federal Reserve Bank that prints paper money with no backing. Consider; a pre 1965 silver dime is now worth over $3.50.

With decreased savings and job-based medical care, workers retired without medical insurance and without adequate savings bringing on the need for Medicare. It, along with Medicaid, was passed in 1965.

Following this, the law of unintended consequences raised its ugly head. Medical care costs began to rapidly rise as a percentage of the economy. This was completely predictable. After all, for patients, medical care seemed free. For doctors, they could raise their fees with impunity. The government responded, and in 1973, Congress passed the Health Maintenance Organization Act, which encouraged managed care. This is where insurance companies make your medical care choices to contain costs. I call this "corporate socialized medicine." In spite of this, medical care costs have sky rocketed to about twenty percent of the economy.

Our system of corporate socialized medicine is the worst of all worlds. It is very expensive. Insurance companies, under government regulation, are controlling the health care choices. We still have the problem of people losing their medical care when they change jobs. We certainly would not think of turning our money over to a car dealer and then asking him to select what car we would drive. I believe that corporate socialized medicine is a corporate welfare system that allows insurance companies and bureaucrats to suck money out of the medical care system.

In conclusion, ObamaCare is just part of the problem. We will continue to have health care problems until we change our tax system and rid ourselves of the Federal Reserve Bank. Chapter 9 discusses how corruption of the Bill of Rights is needed to implement the income tax. Chapter 13 discusses how states could start our return to sound money. Once these things are done, we can begin to move back to a free market health care system.

Chapter 12
ORIGINAL JURISDICTION

Article III, Section II, Clause 2
In all Cases ... and those in which a State shall be Party, the Supreme Court shall have original Jurisdiction.

Most federal cases where a state is a party currently go to lower courts where they are usually decided. This is time consuming and it is expensive as the cases make their way up through the appeal courts.

Resistance
States can insist that in all cases in which they are a party are to be tried only by the Supreme Court. They can refuse to participate in lower court deliberations. They can nullify lower court rulings and injunctions by refusing to obey them.

For instance, there is a twenty year ongoing dispute between Georgia, Alabama, and Florida over the water of the Chattahoochee River. Federal Judge Paul Magnuson is from Minnesota and said that Atlanta cannot use the water.

Because of this lower court ruling, Georgia is in the process of developing new water sources. One source is by building expensive reservoirs. Another supply could come from the Tennessee River. Georgia is in a border dispute with Tennessee that has lasted almost two hundred years.

In both instances, Georgia could claim the right

to be tried only before the Supreme Court. They could claim the lower court ruling of Judge Magnuson to be null and void and not to be followed

One of the main purposes of the Supreme Court was to settle disputes between the states. If this had been argued before the Supreme Court, perhaps there would be a resolution to these expensive water wars.

A state could create legislation declaring that the federal Environmental Protection Agency only had jurisdiction over pollutants that crossed state lines and did not have jurisdiction over the rivers and standing water wetlands in their state. The legislation could say that any federal EPA regulations over wetlands in their state are unconstitutional

It could also say that If the federal EPA filed a compliance order against one of their citizens for a wetland infraction, that their state must be part of that suit. With original jurisdiction, this means rather than enduring the expense and time of going through the lower courts, the case would go directly to the Supreme Court.

Chapter 13
CORRUPTION - MONEY
Corruption is a deviation from the ideal

Article I, Section 10, Clause 1
No State shall ...   make any Thing but gold and silver Coin a Tender in Payment of Debts;

The standard definition of money is a medium of exchange and a store of value.   In a free market money is a commodity like gold and silver coin.   It can also be paper certificates backed by gold and silver coin.

Fiat money is a paper certificate not backed by a commodity. It must be declared legal tender by governments so that people will accept this paper as money. Fiat money has always led to inflation and this often leads to revolution.

The federal government first issued fiat money in 1861 to help fund the Civil War. To have people accept this paper currency as real money, Congress passed and Lincoln signed The Legal Tender Act of 1862. This act said that individuals must accept these paper notes in payment of legal debt.

This was a controversial policy because of the resulting inflation.   Since 1913 when the Federal Reserve Bank was founded, inflation has progressed so that in 2012, a twenty dollar gold coin is worth over $1700.

There is nothing in the Constitution that gives Congress the power to create legal tender laws that force American citizens to accept paper money.

Resistance

It is corruption by state politicians not to adhere to the Constitution and accept only gold and silver or notes backed by gold and silver in payment of debt. If this was done, it would nullify the legal tender laws and could begin to return us to a sound dollar.

States are beginning to introduce legislation to comply with the U.S. Constitution in this matter.

Chapter 14
CORRUPTION - TERM LIMITS
Corruption is a deviation from the ideal

Term limits is one of the most popular issues of the day. In the past, twenty-three states had legislated term limits for Congressional offices. In U.S. Term Limits, Inc. v. Thornton, 1995, the Supreme Court ruled in a five to four split decision that state laws for term limits were unconstitutional. In a five to four split decision, the Court said that the Constitution placed some qualifications on term limits.

Article I, Section 2: **"No Person shall be a Representative who shall not have attained to the Age of twenty-five Years, and been seven Years a Citizen of the United States..."**

Article I, Section 3: **No person shall be a Senator who shall not have attained to the Age of thirty Years, and been nine Years a Citizen of the United States..."**

The five majority lawyers reasoned that because the Constitution put some limits on the members of Congress that the states could not put further qualifications on candidates.

This is a corruption of the Constitution to make this ruling. In a well reasoned dissent, Justice Clarence Thomas said:

Nothing in the Constitution deprives the people of each State of the power to prescribe eligibility requirements for the candidates who seek to represent them in Congress. The Constitution is simply silent on this question. And where the Constitution is silent, it raises no bar to action by the States or the people.

Resistance

The states listed below have federal term limits on their books:

> Alaska, Measure 4 (1994)
> Arkansas Constitution, Amdt. 73, 3
> Arizona Constitution, Art. VII, 18
> Colorado Constitution, Art. XVIII, 9a;
> Florida Constitution, Art. VI, 4(b)(5)
> Michigan Constitution, Art. II, 10;
> Missouri Constitution, Art. III, 45(a);
> Montana Constitution, Art. IV, 8;
> Ohio Constitution, Art. V, 8;
> Oklahoma Constitution, Art. II, 12A;
> South Dakota Constitution, Art. III, 32;

Governors and secretaries of state take an oath to uphold the U.S. Constitution. They should determine if they think the majority opinion was correct or that of the minority led by Justice Thomas. If they believe that the minority opinion was correct, then they are duty bound to nullify this Supreme Court ruling by enforcing their state laws. They should keep the violating federal Representatives and Senators off the ballot.

Chapter 15
CRITICISM OF NULLIFICATION
Nullification would create chaos

It is not the states but the federal government that creates chaos by creating unconstitutional laws. For instance, during the 1973 oil crises, the federal government passed laws that set the speed limit at 55 MPH. After a while, the states began passing their own speed limit laws which effectively nullified the federal laws. Rather than going to war over this, the federal government repealed the federal speed limit laws. It was not the states but the federal government creating chaos by making laws that were not pursuant to the Constitution.

Another example is that federal law makes marijuana sales and possession illegal. There is no logical Constitutional basis for this. In 1992, California legalized medical marijuana. The physicians and patients of California are unsure of the legality of their actions when medical marijuana is prescribed. It is not the states but the federal government creating unconstitutional laws that creates this chaos.

Nullification is Racist

In his speech on August 28, 1963, Dr.Martin Luther King, Jr. said:

I have a dream that one day down in Alabama with its vicious racists, with its governor having his lips dripping with the words of interposition and nullification, one day right there in Alabama little black boys and black girls will be able to join hands with little white boys and white girls as sisters and brothers.

Dr. King is correct that Governor George Wallace said he would refuse to obey federal law. In his January 14, 1963, inaugural address, Wallace said, "Segregation now, segregation tomorrow, segregation forever."

The Fourteenth Amendment gave a new power to the federal government. It gave it the power to rule state laws unconstitutional:

No State shall make or enforce any law which shall abridge the privileges or immunities of citizens of the United States; nor shall any State deprive any person of life, liberty, or property, without due process of law; nor deny to any person within its jurisdiction the equal protection of the laws.

The original intent of the Fourteenth Amendment was to assure that all Americans, regardless of their race, sex, or sexual orientation, were treated equally by the law. Until the Civil Rights movement, this was not done because of the Jim Crow laws of "separate but equal." In Plessy v. Ferguson (1896), the Supreme Court was corrupt in ruling "separate but equal" was constitutional.

It was the Supreme Court that had failed to nullify the unconstitutional state segregation laws.

George Wallace was doing what had been done in the past. The civil rights movement and courageous African Americans, like Dr. Martin Luther King, nullified these unconstitutional state laws by civil disobedience. The state laws were unconstitutional because the African Americans were treated separately than the whites. This violated the original intent of the Fourteenth Amendment.

Today, the original intent of the Fourteenth Amendment has been corrupted because it is being used to further move the United States away from the original intent of our Constitution, which was federalism.

Times are Different

Madison said that factions controlling a strong central government would lead to violence. His principle that the way to control the factions with a federation is timeless.

History has shown that central control of the economy and the people leads to poverty and misery for the majority of the people. It often leads to war.

How would you Control pollution?

Economic freedom leads to prosperity and this leads to people desiring a clean environment. There would be state and local regulations to control pollution. There are federal courts to arbitrate when one state pollutes another state.

There is a possibility that the federal EPA is constitutional if it restrains itself to only controlling pollution that crosses state lines. For instance, a state could have a factory that is polluting a river. When the river enters another state, the EPA could tell the polluting state that it has to stop polluting the river. It would then be up to the polluting state to regulate the factory.

The States Could Never Manage

Consider gambling and prostitution. These are two areas in which the federal government has not produced laws if it is within state borders. Each state has its own laws on these issues and neither of these moral issues have widespread problems like the federal war on drugs. This is not to say that all states have good laws. It does say that as a whole, the states can handle most issues better and with less problems than the federal government.

It WIll Never Happen

It is already happening. The unconstitutional federal Real ID Act was passed in 2005. The states have responded with various non cooperation legislations causing the federal government to delay implementation of the law.

Patients are legally using medical marijuana in many states despite conflicting federal laws.

We have a Living Constitution

If this means that we have an amendment process to allow for change, then we have a living constitution.

If this means that Congress, The President, and The Supreme Court can collude to change the Constitution on a whim, then we have a dead constitution.

Nullification Violates
The Supremacy Clause

When people argue for the Supremacy Clause, they always leave out, **"In Pursuance thereof."** An unconstitutional law is not the supreme law of the land. States, and local governments can judge if a federal law is constitutional. When they do, they are duty bound to declare it null and void and unenforceable.

The Civil War settled that

This is about a contract dispute, not secession and war. Do critics of nullification really suggest they we should go to war over such things as data collection on a drivers license or marijuana use?

The Supreme Court is Infallible

Not only does the Constitution not say that the Supreme Court is infallible. It says that Congress may regulate The Supreme Court: Article III, Section 2, Clause 2 says, **"In all the other Cases before mentioned, the supreme Court shall have appellate Jurisdiction, both as to Law and Fact, with such Exceptions, and under such Regulations as the Congress shall make."**

Perhaps the time has come for Congress to assert this constitutional power.

Federalism is Inefficient
Judge the tree by the fruit it bears

The federal government has unconstitutionally created a de facto fourth branch of government. These are the regulatory agencies that create the rules, enforce the rules, and judge the rules. There are hundreds of these agencies, which are costly and inefficient. Every regulation increases the cost of doing businesses and increases the price for customers.

Chapter 16
WE HAVE MET THE ENEMY
AND HE IS US

This quote is from Pogo, the cartoon character created by the cartoonist, Walt Kelly. It expresses one of the problems with the Nullification movement. When there is a local problem, people form a faction to try to fix it. One way to fix it is to go to a federal agency to seek help. Clear cutting of government lands is controversial. Critics say it is a government revenue enhancer and because of fire suppression policies, it is needed for the health of the land. Others see the ugliness it produces and disagree. They form factions to stop it.

These factions will approach their cause in different ways. One way is to seek help from the federal EPA. They argue that clear cutting pollutes the streams with dirty runoff water and this violates the Clean Water Act. This runs contrary to the nullification movement.

A better approach is to question the Constitutionality of the federal government owning national forests. The power to do this is not in the seventeen powers that the states gave to Congress.

The federal government claims it owns sixty percent of the land in the state of Utah, but Utah challenges this. It is fighting back with an eminent domaine bill to reclaim their land. This became law in 2010 but the governor and attorney general have never attempted to occupy the national forests in Utah.

Many conservatives deplore the poor quality of education in our public school systems and often blame poor teachers for this. To fix this, some advocate for the federal government to establish national standards. The idea is that those students with the best grades would have the best teachers who should be compensated accordingly. This has produced teachers teaching to the tests rather than educating their students.

This is conservatives advocating for national solutions. The nullification movement would say that the powers given to Congress in Article I, Section 8, Clause 3 did not include making laws or creating agencies concerning education. The movement would say that states and local school boards setting the education standards would do a better job. The national standard would not be uniform but on average would be better than the current system.

Chapter 17
A WINNING STRATEGY

The Nullification Movement is a Big Tent

Libertarians believe that free markets and free people will create the most just society. Perhaps they are right, but it would strengthen their cause if they joined the nullification movement. Once the solutions are moved to the state level, libertarians will have a better chance of advancing their ideas.

Progressives believe that government regulations and the welfare state will create the most just society. Conservatives believe that government control of morality and proper administration of the regulatory agencies will lead to the most just society. Both should not be so arrogant to believe their ideas are the best. Both should embrace the opportunity to try their ideas out at the state level.

The nullification movement needs to embrace all types of political persuasions.

It Will Take Time

Many people worry that states nullifying unconstitutional laws could lead to a breakdown in the rule of law, that many of these laws and agencies are necessary, and that each state making their own laws will leave big voids in needed regulations. They worry about the possible conflict between the states and the federal government.

These arguments may have some merit. The nullification movement will take time and should begin with unpopular federal laws. This has already begun with the Real ID Act. This requires states to meet federal standards by having biometric and other data on drivers licenses. At least 25 states have nullified the Real ID Act with laws of non cooperation.

This continues with the legalization of medical marijuana. Recent polls showed that 76 percent of Americans do not want the federal government to force federal anti-marijuana laws on the states. The federal government is beginning to debate changing some of their anti marijuana laws to conform with state laws and public opinion.

It would probably be counterproductive to try to nullify some of the needed laws such as banning lead in gasoline. However, it would be prudent to make sure that each state has needed parallel anti-pollutant laws. Much as the IRS violates the Bill of Rights, states trying to nullify its collection methods could lead to significant confrontation. Individuals fighting the IRS might demand jury trials and use the jury nullification defense.

As nullification progresses, we can make necessary changes in the U.S. Constitution through the amendment process.

The issue is never the issue.
The issue is always the revolution

This quote is from Saul Alinsky's classic book, *Rules for Radicals*. Alinsky was a brilliant man whom many consider to be the founder of modern community organizing.

Alinsky's "revolution" was central control. The

issues of clean air, civil rights, or gun control was not the major issue. The major issue was that each of these issues would be controlled by the central government. Even better would be world government. He believed this would lead to prosperity and equality.

Alinsky's ideology of central control is winning. Most federally elected officials of both parties agree with central control. The conflict between the two parties in Washington is who can run the regulatory state the best.

The nullification movement should embrace Alinsky's idea, but the movement's "revolution" would be for a federation instead of central control. The nullification movement should not take stands on the issues. For the Nullification movement:

The issue is never the issue.
The issue is always decentralization

The Constitution is the Way

Today, the special interest groups and their money control the federal government. There is little expectation that the federal government will change but there is hope. One of the federal government's perceived strengths is central control, but because of our Constitution this is also a weakness. To carry out their plans, they must have the cooperation of the lower levels of government.

The officials of these lower levels of government take an oath to support the U.S. Constitution, not the rulings of the Supreme Court.

The Constitution is the supreme law of the land, but only for laws pursuant to the Constitution. State and local officials are bound by their oath to declare unconstitutional federal laws to be null and void and not to be followed. This is called nullification. They are also bound by their oath to protect their citizens from the unconstitutional laws and regulations of the federal government. This is called interposition.

In the coming years, it is very important for patriotic citizens to become aware of nullification and interposition. For the movement to return us to a federation, we must elect state and local politicians who will uphold their oath to support the U.S. Constitution.